Play It!

LEVEL 1

A Superfast Way to Learn Awesome Music
on Your Piano or Keyboard

CLASSICAL MUSIC

By Jennifer Kemmeter and Antimo Marrone

GRAPHIC ARTS
BOOKS®

Library of Congress Control Number: 2019951433

ISBN: 9781513262482 (paperback) | 9781513262499 (hardbound) | 9781513262505 (e-book)

Proudly distributed by Ingram Publisher Services.

Published by Graphic Arts Books
an imprint of West Margin Press

WEST
MARGIN
PRESS

WestMarginPress.com

WEST MARGIN PRESS
Publishing Director: Jennifer Newens
Marketing Manager: Angela Zbornik
Editor: Olivia Ngai
Design & Production: Rachel Lopez Metzger

Contents

Hi Kids! My Name is Zooey. I'm going to teach you how to play music. Using my awesome system, you don't need to know anything fancy or very technical—all you need is to know your colors, be able to follow a tune, and maybe even sing along. It's easy! Once you learn my cool, color-coded system, you'll be able to play a bunch of songs you probably already recognize, just by pressing the colors on the keyboard. Let's play!

Good Piano Posture
also known as The Pro's Pose!

It may not seem important at first, but when you
sit down to play, the way you sit on the bench or chair
plays a part in how good your music sounds.
Follow this diagram to look and sound like a pro:

1. Let your upper arms hang loose and relaxed from your shoulder.

2. Keep your back straight and lean forward slightly.

3. You want your elbows slightly higher than the keyboard to
   get the best sound from the keys (you may need to adjust the
   seat height or sit on a book to get things just right).

4. Sit on the front half of the bench or chair so that your
   weight is positioned forward toward the keyboard.

5. Position yourself so that your knees are slightly underneath
   the keyboard.

6. Keep your feet flat on the floor. If they don't touch, put some
   books or a step underneath them.

7. Use rounded hands to strike the keys—hold your wrists above
   the keyboard and arch your fingers down toward the keys.

That's it! Now you look like a rock star!

How to Use This Book

Now that you look cool at the keyboard, you're just five steps away from playing your first song! Here's how:

1 **Cut out the color-coded labels** on page 63 or 65. Be sure to set aside the red "Middle C" label, because this one is special. The letters on the labels represent the musical notes on the keyboard. So, red labels represent C notes in music; yellow labels represent E notes; blue labels represent G notes; etcetera.

    TIP: To make the labels last longer, ask your parent or teacher to laminate the sheet of labels before cutting them.

2 **Attach the "Middle C" label to the keyboard.** It's the one nearest the center of the keyboard that's shaped like an "L". You can use tape or removable blue putty to secure the label.

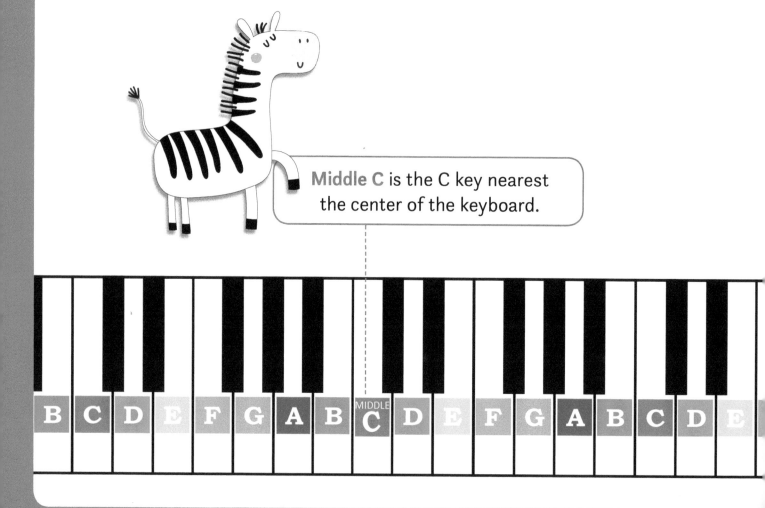

Middle C is the C key nearest the center of the keyboard.

B C D E F G A B MIDDLE C D E F G A B C D E

3 Once you have attached the Middle C, **follow the diagram** on the top of the pages for the song you want to play to attach the rest of the color-coded labels.

TIP: *Put any loose labels into a covered container and tuck them into a drawer or your piano bench for storage.*

The Itsy Bitsy Spider

4 Again referring to the diagram, **place your hands in the correct position** for playing the song. Then, shift your attention to the song and begin to play, pressing the keys with the colors and using the correct finger as shown.

Twinkle, Twinkle Little Star

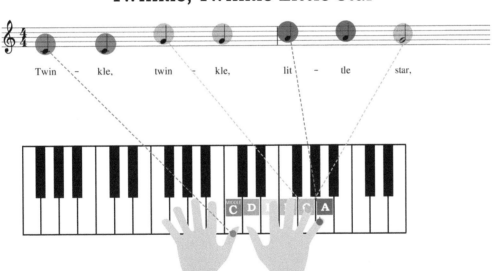

Twin - kle, twin - kle, lit - tle star,

5 **Have fun!** Once you get the hang of it, you'll be able to play a ton of new songs. Look for me throughout the book—I'll be giving you extra tips and tricks so you'll become even more of a rock star as you go.

Let's Get Started!

Before you dive in and play your first song, I want to tell you about a few things you're going to see in the pages that follow.

First, you'll notice that each song is shown on a series of five horizontal lines. This set of lines is called a **staff**. You don't need to worry about this yet—your focus will be on the colors—but the music notes get placed on the staff and represent specific keys on the piano.

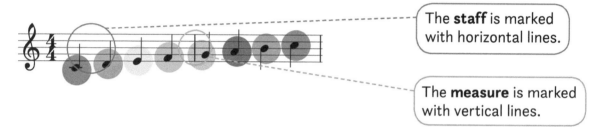

The **staff** is marked with horizontal lines.

The **measure** is marked with vertical lines.

Next, the staff is divided into individual sections, each separated by a vertical line. Each section between the vertical lines is called a **measure**. These measures help divide the song into smaller bits that make it easier to learn how to play.

There's also something called the **time signature**. The time signature tells you how to count the music.

 The top number tells you how many beats are in each measure. (Ignore the bottom number for now.)

For example, if you see: there are 4 beats in the measure

 there are 3 beats in the measure

 there are 2 beats in the measure

Time to Warm Up!

Professional rock stars always warm up before their gigs.
Here's a cool way for you to warm up too—the scale.

1 Follow the diagram below to attach the color-coded labels to the keyboard.

2 Starting with your left pinkie and ending with your right pinkie, play each colored key one at a time.

3 Do the same thing again, only backwards: start with your right pinkie and play each note until you reach your left pinkie.

4 Repeat steps 2 and 3 a few times until your fingers feel nice and loose. Do this every time you sit down at the keyboard.

Now, let's try some exercises.

Exercise 1

Good to know: If you see a note that looks like

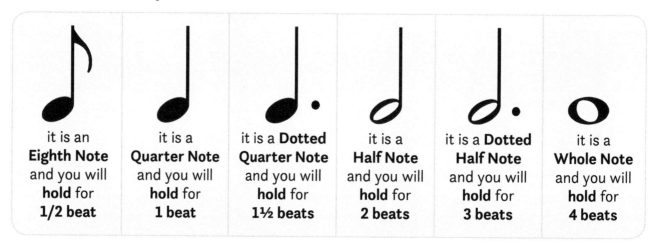

| it is an **Eighth Note** and you will **hold** for **1/2 beat** | it is a **Quarter Note** and you will **hold** for **1 beat** | it is a **Dotted Quarter Note** and you will **hold** for **1½ beats** | it is a **Half Note** and you will **hold** for **2 beats** | it is a **Dotted Half Note** and you will **hold** for **3 beats** | it is a **Whole Note** and you will **hold** for **4 beats** |

Now you try: Clap out the **rhythm** and **sing**

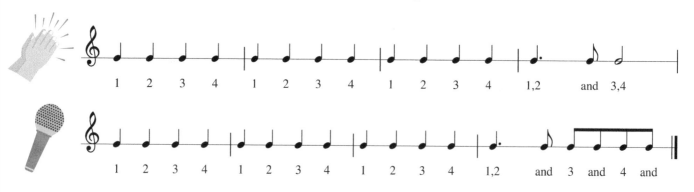

Start to play: Using your right hand, practice the notes you will play.

RESTING   PLAYING

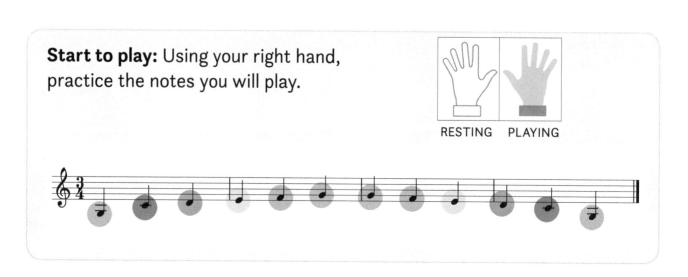

Got it? Good. Let's try playing some pieces.

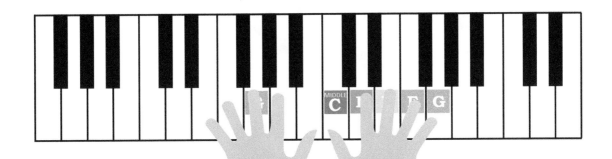

Ode to Joy LUDWIG VAN BEETHOVEN

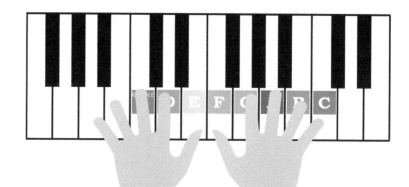

Lullaby Johannes Brahms

Spring from *The Four Seasons* Antonio Vivaldi

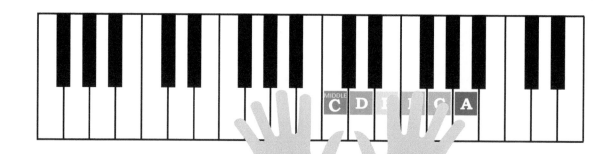

Serenade No. 2 in A Major   Johannes Brahms

Exercise 2

Remember: The notes are placed on the staff in a specific way.

The notes in the **spaces** spell

F A C E

Say it 5 times: *"If it's in a space, it's part of FACE."*

The notes in the **lines**

E G B D F

can be remembered in a sentence:

"Every Good Boy Deserves Fudge."

Say it 5 times: *"Every Good Boy Deserves Fudge."*

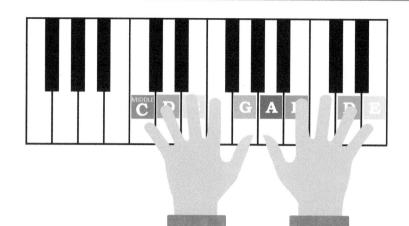

Jimbo's Lullaby CLAUDE DEBUSSY

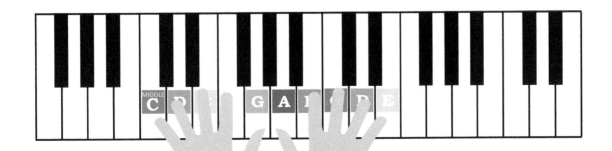

Largo from Symphony No. 9 ANTONIN DVORAK

Exercise 3

Play with the correct finger:
Sometimes you will need to move your hand to reach the keys. We number the fingers to show you how to play.

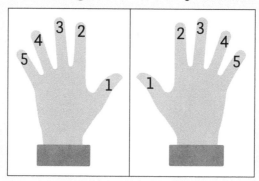

Sharps ♯ and **Flats** ♭

Have you noticed that we're only playing on the white keys? Well, the black keys can also be played. They are called **sharps** and **flats**.

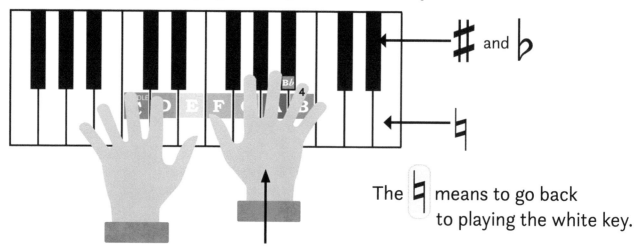

♯ and ♭

♮

The ♮ means to go back to playing the white key.

Move your hand forward so your finger can reach the black keys.

Practice moving your hand ↑ and ↓ to go between ♭ and ♮

Symphony No. 8 — Ludwig van Beethoven

Can-Can from *Orphée aux Enfers* JACQUES OFFENBACH

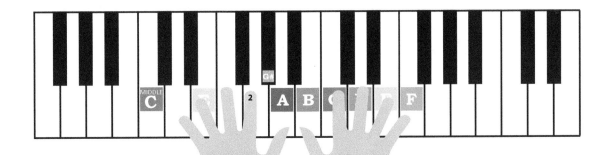

Rondo from *Orchestral Suite No. 2* Johann Sebastian Bach

Quiz Time!

Don't worry, you've got this!

Name the **notes** below.

C   D   __ __ __ __ __ __ __ __ __ __ __ __ __ __ __ __

__ __ __ __ __ __ __ __ __ __ __ __ __ __ __ __

How many **beats** does each play for?

1   1   __ __ __ __ __ __ __

__ __ __ __ __ __ __ __ __ __ __ __

Complete the sentence:

"If it's in a space, it's part of _____"

"Every good boy _____ _____"

Air on a G String JOHANN SEBASTIAN BACH

A triplet is 3 notes in 1 beat

When you see this symbol

Hold for 1, 2, 3, 4, 5

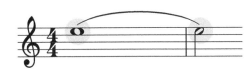

Exercise 4

NEW! Changing the hand positions: **Stretching**
Sometimes you won't need to fully slide your hand to reach a key,
you need to **stretch** the hand wide for the pinky to reach.

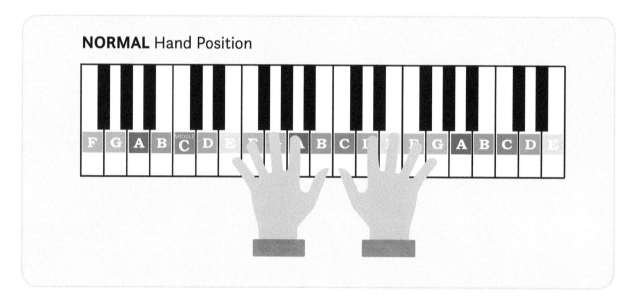

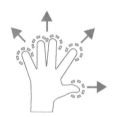

Stretch your hand to reach more keys.

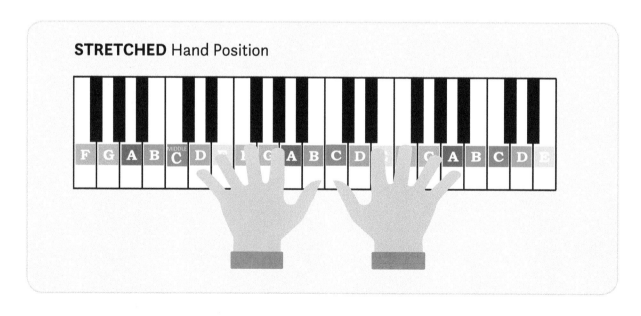

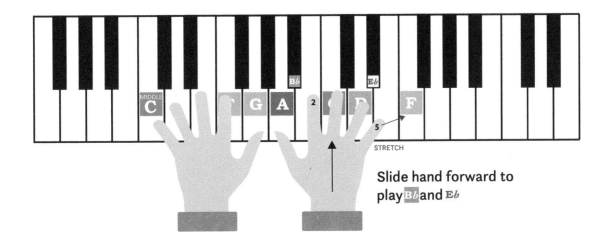

Bridal Chorus from *Lohengrin* RICHARD WAGNER

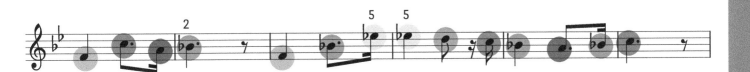

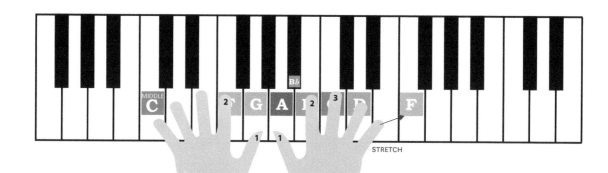

Cradle Song (Wiegenlied)

WOLFGANG AMADEUS MOZART

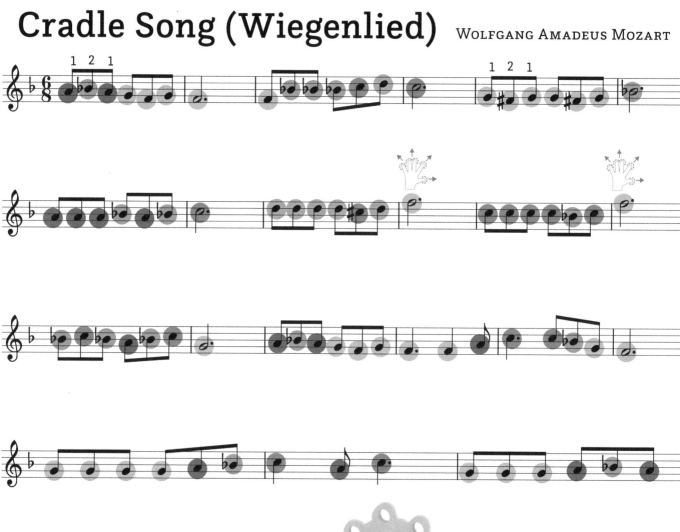

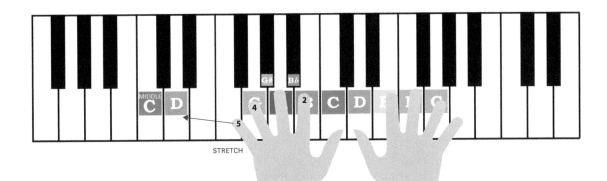

Fantaisie Impromptu FREDERIC CHOPIN

Exercise 5

NEW! Naming the hand positions: Hand position is named for the key the thumb is on.

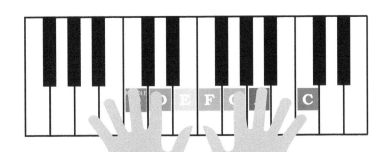

"The left hand is in **E** position."

"The right hand is in **F** position."

"The left hand is in **B** position."

"The right hand is in **C** position."

"The left hand is in **G** position."

"The right hand is in **A** position."

Quiz Time!

Don't worry, you've got this!
Name the **hand positions** on the keyboards below.

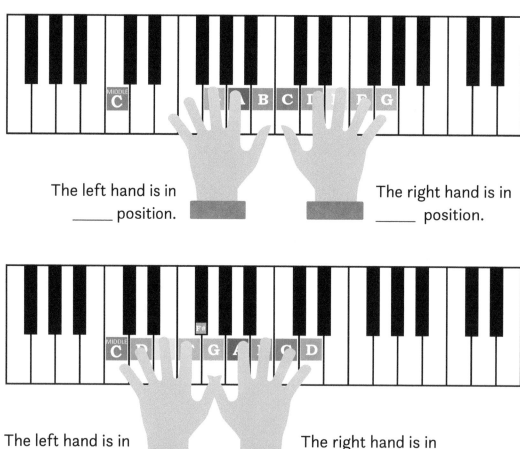

The left hand is in
_____ position.

The right hand is in
_____ position.

The left hand is in
_____ position.

The right hand is in
_____ position.

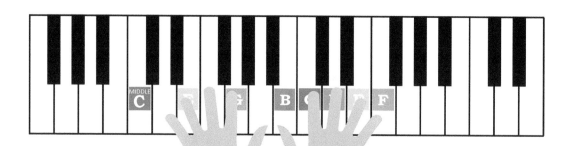

The left hand is in
_____ position.

The right hand is in
_____ position.

Exercise 6

NEW! Changing the hand positions:
Hands can move up and down the full keyboard by walking your first three fingers up and down the keyboard.

Your thumb will go under finger 3 as you "walk" up the keyboard. (Remember to press the black keys too!)

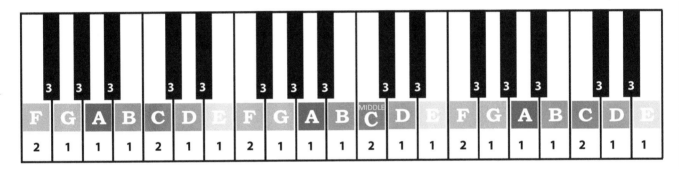

 Cross a thumb under a finger going up (to the right)

Cross finger over thumb going down (to the left)

Now you try: Walk your right hand up and down the keyboard by crossing one finger over another again and again using the diagram above. Remember to use your middle finger on the black keys!

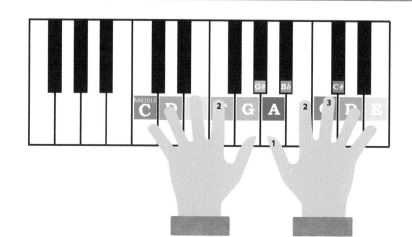

Song of the Toreador from *Carmen*

GEORGES BIZET

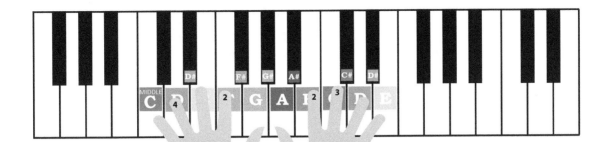

Die Fledermaus JOHANN STRAUSS II

Glockenspiel from *The Magic Flute*

WOLFGANG AMADEUS MOZART

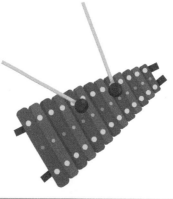

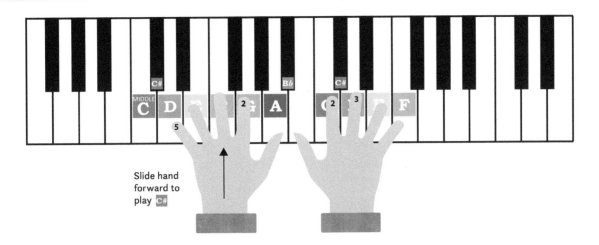

Minuet in D Minor JOHANN SEBASTIAN BACH

Exercise 7

Changing the hand positions: Jumping
Sometimes if one hand is playing and the other resting, the resting hand will **jump** over the other to help play the notes.

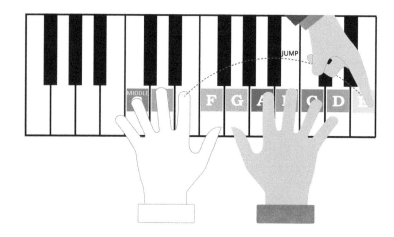

Practice the following exercise, with the left hand jumping back and forth over the right to play the notes for **Allegro from Eine Kleine Nachtmusik** (see page 39).

JUMP

1. Practice the jumped musical phrase **5 times**.

2. Pay attention to the position of your thumb, so you can return to the original hand position easily.

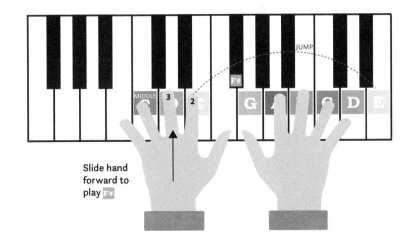

Allegro from Eine Kleine Nachtmusik

WOLFGANG AMADEUS MOZART

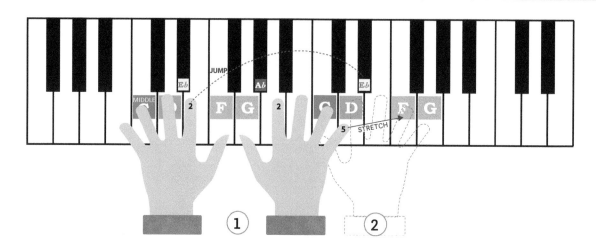

Symphony No. 5 LUDWIG VAN BEETHOVEN

Learn about sliding your hand on page 46!

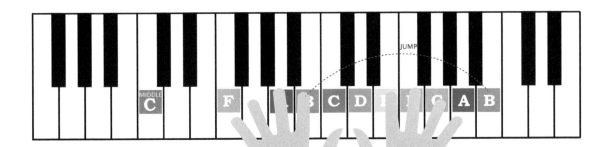

Swan Lake PYOTR TCHAIKOVSKY

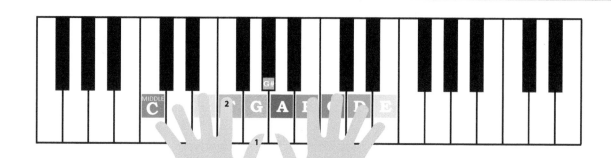

Turkish March LUDWIG VAN BEETHOVEN

Strike accented
notes loudly

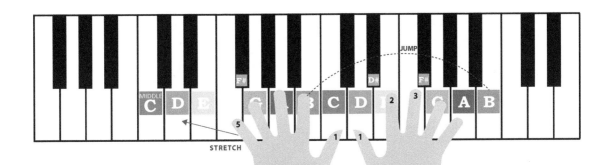

Gavotte GEORG FRIEDRICH HANDEL

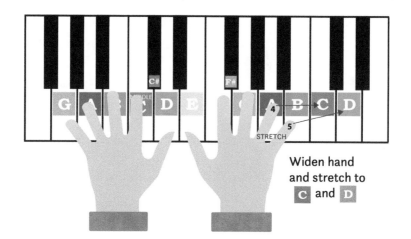

Widen hand
and stretch to
C and **D**

Brandenburg Concerto No. 3 Johann Sebastian Bach

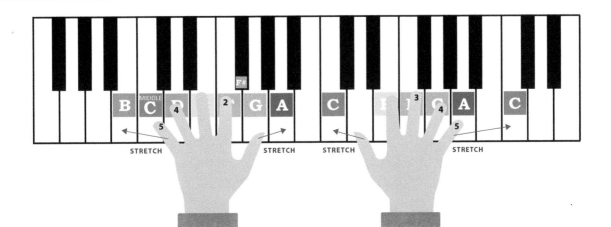

The Blue Danube JOHANN STRAUSS II

Exercise 8

NEW! Changing the hand positions: **Sliding**
Sometimes you will **slide** your hands up (to the right)
or down (to the left) the keyboard to play the notes.

In the example below, hands move together so both thumbs go up **two keys**.
Left thumb **C** to **E** , right thumb **D** to **F**. The other fingers follow.

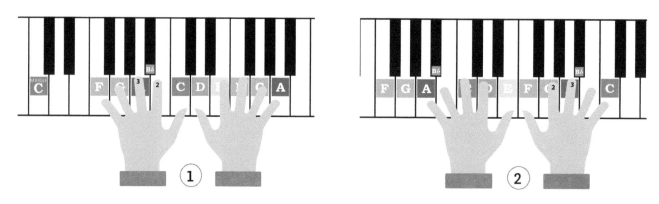

1 Move your hands together.

2 Pay attention to the position of your thumbs, and keep them
on keys next to each other when possible.

Practice playing the notes for **Intermezzo No. 1** on page 47.

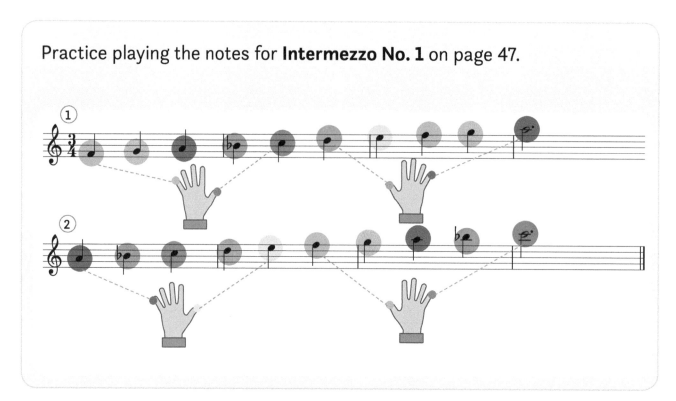

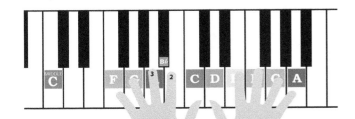

Move hands position
2 keys to the right

Intermezzo No. 1 Johannes Brahms

Move hands position
3 keys to the right

Minuet from Don Giovanni WOLFGANG AMADEUS MOZART

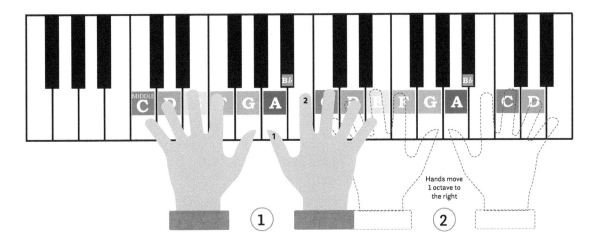

La Donna è mobile JOHANN SEBASTIAN BACH

② Play the same line, 1 octave higher

② Same line as above, except the last 2 measures

1 octave is 8 notes or keys.

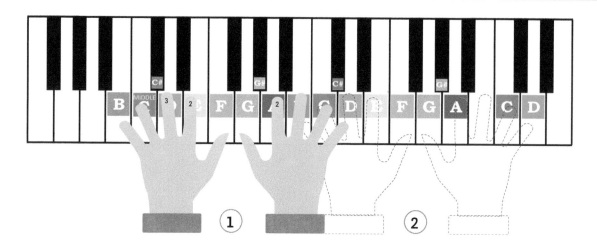

Sonata Pathetique LUDWIG VAN BEETHOVEN

Move left hand
1 octave up

Move right hand
1 octave up

Move hands position
3 keys to the right

Over the Waves JUVENTINO ROSAS

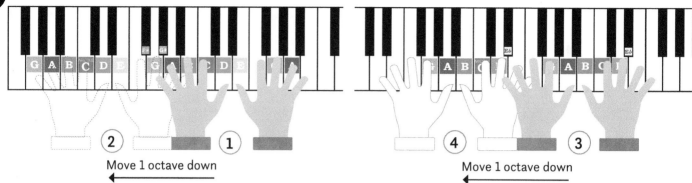

Morning from *Peer Gynt* EDVARD GRIEG

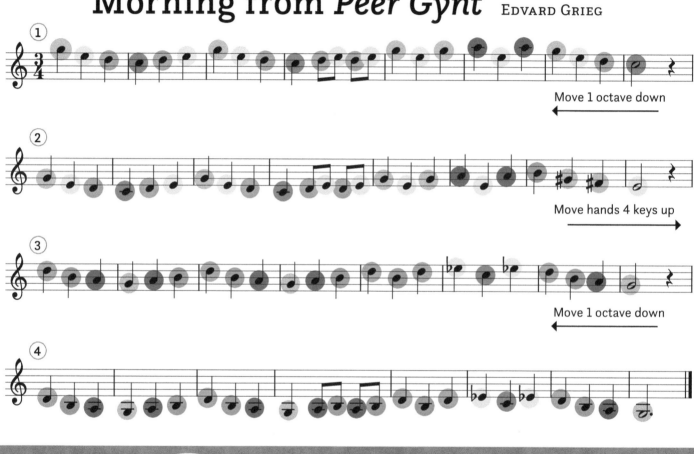

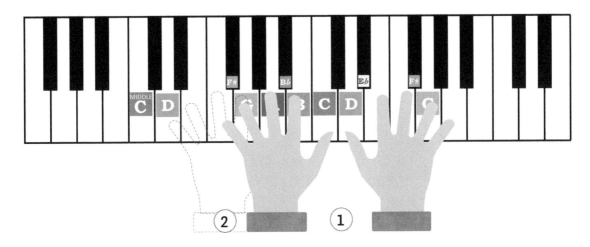

Bagatelle in G Minor, Op. 119, No.1 Ludwig van Beethoven

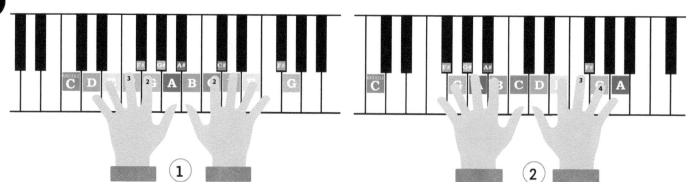

Minuet in G LUDWIG VAN BEETHOVEN

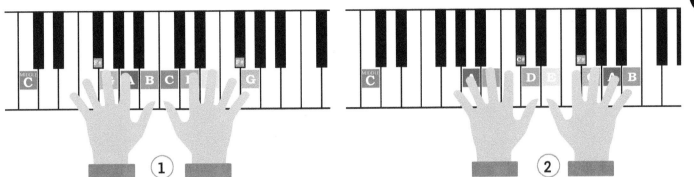

Minuet in G Johann Sebastian Bach

William Tell Overture GIOACHINO ROSSINI

Exercise 9

NEW! You might notice on the songs that follow some strange symbols called **clefs.** Here's what they do:

F CLEF

G CLEF

← Left hand plays to

Right hand plays to →

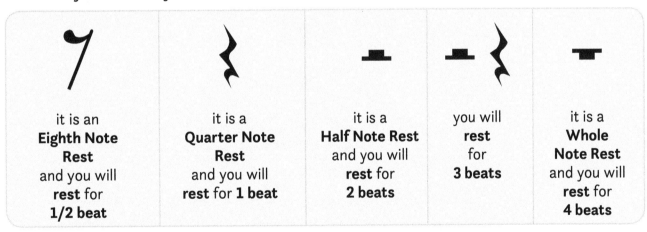

The dots of the "F clef" or "bass clef" are above and below the line that marks the F note on the staff.

The "G clef" or "treble clef" curls around the line that marks the G note on the staff.

NEW! If you see a symbol that look like

it is an **Eighth Note Rest** and you will **rest** for **1/2 beat**	it is a **Quarter Note Rest** and you will **rest** for **1 beat**	it is a **Half Note Rest** and you will **rest** for **2 beats**	you will **rest** for **3 beats**	it is a **Whole Note Rest** and you will **rest** for **4 beats**

For every song that follows, start with the following **warm-up:**

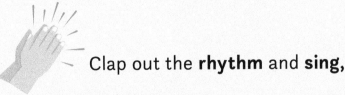

Clap out the **rhythm** and **sing,**

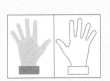

then practice the **notes** you will play on each hand.

Exercise 10

Remember: The notes are placed on the staff in a specific way.

On the **G clef,** the notes in the **spaces** spell

F A C E

Say it 5 times: *"If it's in a space, it's part of FACE."*

On the **G clef,** the notes in the **lines**

E G B D F

can be remembered in a sentence:

"Every Good Boy Deserves Fudge."

Say it 5 times: *"Every Good Boy Deserves Fudge."*

NEW! On the **F clef,** the notes in the **spaces**

A C E G

can be remembered in a sentence:

"All Cows Eat Grass."

Say it 5 times: *"All Cows Eat Grass."*

NEW! On the **F clef,** the notes in the **lines**

G B D F A

can be remembered in a sentence:

"Good Bikes Don't Fall Apart."

Say it 5 times: *"Good Bikes Don't Fall Apart."*

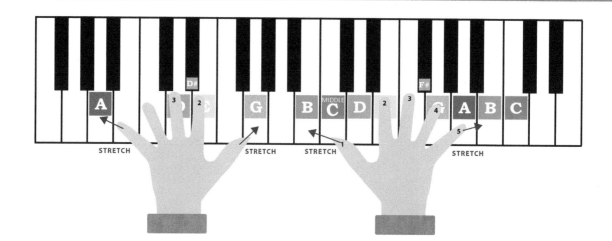

Moonlight Sonata Ludwig van Beethoven

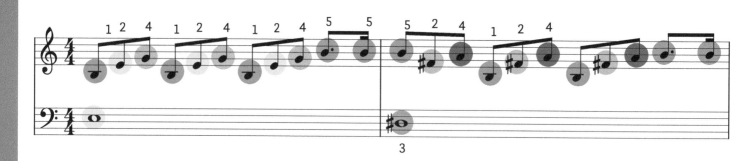

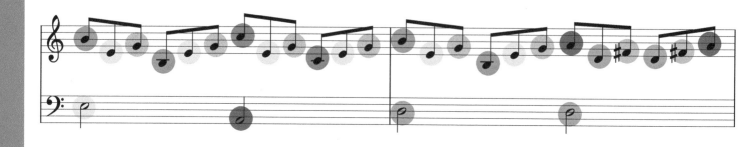

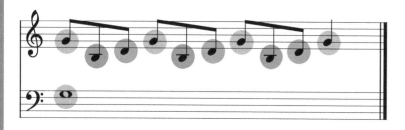

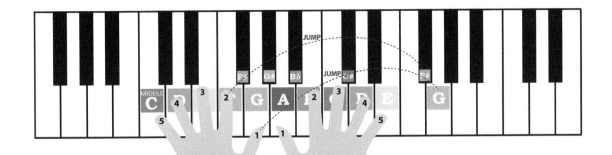

Habanera from *Carmen* GEORGES BIZET

Cut the labels below and attach them to your piano keys as shown on page 8.

Standard size piano key labels

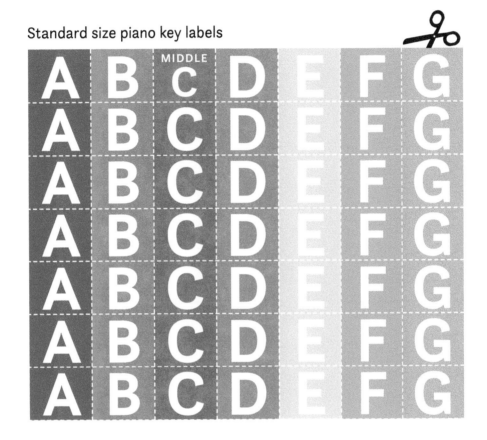

Mini key labels

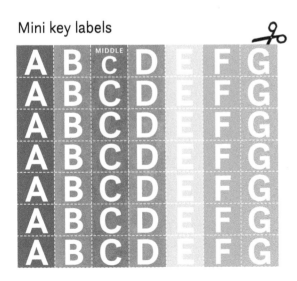

Mid-size piano key labels

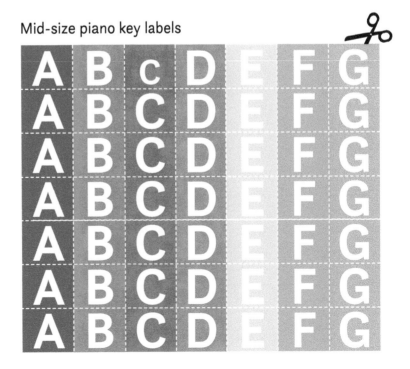

Cut the labels below and attach them to your piano keys as shown on page 8.

Standard size piano key labels

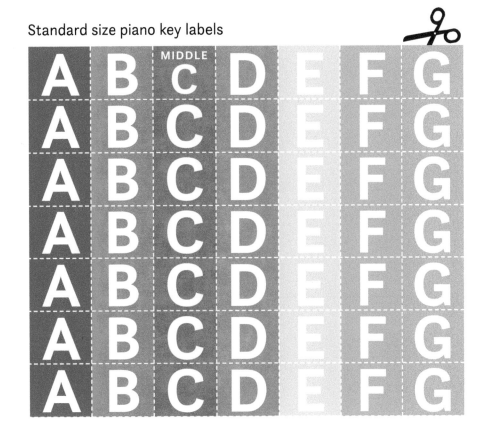

Mini key labels

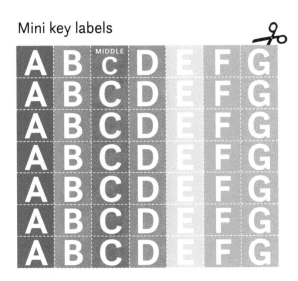

Mid-size piano key labels

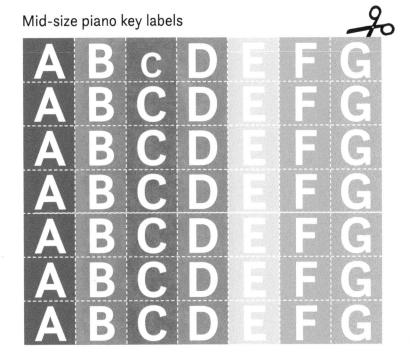

Congratulations!

_____
(your name)

worked hard
and finished

Play It!
LEVEL 1

CLASSICAL MUSIC

Make sure your
Play It!
library is complete